zendoodle col

Enchanting Gardens

Other great books in the series
zendoodle coloring

Calming Swirls

Creative Sensations

Inspiring Zendalas

zendoodle coloring
Enchanting Gardens
Captivating Florals to Color and Display

illustrations by
Nikolett Corley

ST. MARTIN'S GRIFFIN
NEW YORK

ZENDOODLE COLORING: ENCHANTING GARDENS.
Copyright © 2015 by St. Martin's Press. All rights reserved.
Printed in the United States of America. For information, address
St. Martin's Press, 175 Fifth Avenue, New York, N.Y. 10010.

www.stmartins.com

ISBN 978-1-250-08646-4 (trade paperback)

St. Martin's Griffin books may be purchased for educational, business, or promotional use. For information on bulk purchases, please contact the Macmillan Corporate and Premium Sales Department at 1-800-221-7945, extension 5442, or write to specialmarkets@macmillan.com.

First Edition: July 2015

10 9 8 7 6 5